DOWN FOR THE COUNT

Bouncing Back from Life's Blows

Compiled by Felicia C. Lucas

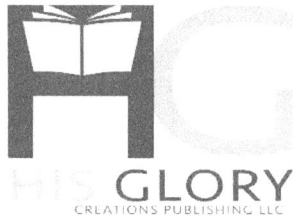

HIS GLORY
CREATIONS PUBLISHING LLC

www.hisglorycreationspublishing.com

Scripture references are used with permission from Zondervan via Biblegateway.com

ISBN: 978-1-7327227-0-5
Library of Congress Number: 2018910720

Published by: His Glory Creations Publishing, LLC

Scripture references are used with permission from Zondervan via Biblegateway.com

Cover Photo: Pixabay.com

Printed in the United States of America

FELICIA C. LUCAS

This book is dedicated to individuals who are facing impossible situations and are seeking some inspiration in order to make it through the storm.

ACKNOWLEDGEMENTS

AUTHOR FELICIA LUCAS

Thank you to my husband, children, family and friends who have consistently supported me on my literary journey. I appreciate each of you. To my editor, Angela McClain of AM Editing, thank you for your professional services. To my co-authors, thank you for participating in this project and having the courage to share your stories. Each of you are phenomenal and I am so excited about this journey we are taking together. To my His Glory Creations Publishing LLC team, thank you for everything! You Rock!

AUTHOR CHRISTINE WILSON

From start to finish I thank my Lord and Savior Jesus Christ for favoring me to experience so many wonderful things. His loving kindness and tender mercies keep me in a state of perpetual worship. To my best friend, love of my life, priest of our home; my husband, Andrew Wilson. Even when I sat in the corner trying to fade into the background, you believed in me and have been an integral part of my arriving at this place in life. Thank you Love. To the visionary of this work, Felicia Lucas. "Eye has not seen, nor ear heard, nor have entered into the heart of man the things which God has prepared for those who love Him." Bless you!

AUTHOR DETRA WILLIAMS

My chapter is dedicated to all the Survivors and Overcomers of child molestation, sexual and physical abuse, who made it out and those that are currently going through domestic violence. To my son's Andra' and Leland, you guys are such an inspiration to me, through all you have witnessed as it relates to abuse, you did not let your past destroy who you have become. I love you and continue to be the God-fearing men that God made you to be. To my mother Vivian, there is so much I can say, one thing for sure, YOU TOO ARE A SURVIVOR. The release of the first book allowed us to talk openly about the elements of the past. Thank you for understanding that this was God's plan and things happened the way it should have. To my step-father Charles, you were there from the beginning of the physical abuse, and you came to my rescue every time, and I greatly appreciate the love you have for me. To my beloved husband, the late Johnnie Lee Williams, the Lord whispered into his ear and called him home on 11-18-17. I will forever be grateful for the positive impact and for the love he had given me for the past 20 years. His death has showed me that God can open a chapter in your life and at the same time close one as well. I hurt, I cry, but I also smile because my love had the chance to see my dream come forth. He never read my story because he heard the pain I endured, personally from me. He said that he did not have to read it because he saw the results of God's Greatness. Rest in Heaven, my dear.

AUTHOR NICHOLE BOBBITT

First, I want to thank the Lord. Secondly, I want to thank my mom (Eve High) who said I could do it. I want to send some big shout outs to Sharlrita Deloatch, and Latausah Roberts. I also would like to thank Glendora Adkin, for always believing in me. And finally a great big shout out to Felicia Lucas who would not let me give up!

FELICIA C. LUCAS

AUTHOR DIANE PACE

I would like to express my gratitude to the many people who saw me through this book; I thank God. I would like to thank my publisher, Felicia Lucas for enabling me to publish this chapter. I would like to thank my mother Frances Turner, the late Bishop Sylvester Holder, his wife the late Ruby Holder, & their daughter the late Wilma Jean Holder for being great leaders in my Christian foundation. It really inspired me in writing my chapter. Thank you, Julia Walker, for your support. Thank you to my daughter Renee Walker who prayed & encouraged me every step of the way. Above all I want to thank my husband, Raymond Pace for his love, support & encouragement.

AUTHOR PAMELA CARROLL

I would like to give thanks to my parents Jesse and Bessie Jones, who have helped me through the hard times. Every word that was shared with me has never gone unheard. I give thanks to my children and that God gives you blessings which are needed at the appropriate time. Latoria, you were my endurance; Jesse, you are my heart; Andrea, you were my joy; and Damaris, you were my strength. My husband James Carroll, when you held my hand, I knew I was now safe and where I was supposed to be. You all have given a reason for my light to shine!

AUTHOR SHONTE MONROE

First I would like to thank God for making all things possible in my life! I trust him and love him with my whole heart! To my mommy the Late Grace A. Monroe, who will forever live in my heart, I thank her for speaking life into me so many times and for teaching me how to be successful in everything I do. I would like to thank my daddy Leon Monroe my biggest miracle and blessing. Thanks for always being by my side. To my Pastor Dr. Damieon L. Royal and Lady Royal and to my church family, thanks for your support and many prayers! To the love of my life Freddie, thanks for being my rock and supporting me 100% and also for sticking with me through the good and bad times. Lastly, I would like to thank my family and friends and my support system for the love and support all of you have shown towards me. God bless you all!!! Thanks so much you, are appreciated!!!

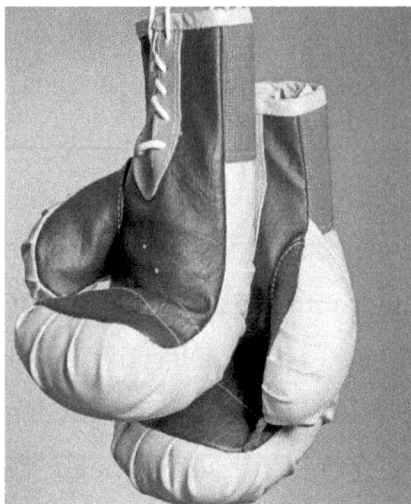

Table of Contents

INTRODUCTION

By Felicia C. Lucas

Over the course of my life, I have often thought about the story of Job in the Bible. Job was an upright man who experienced extreme levels of adversity in his life to include losing everything in which he was closely connected to. Even as he was going through his experiences, he had a tremendous level of faith and even expressed it to God by saying in Job 13:15 (King James Version)" Though he slay me, yet will I trust in him." Now that is a powerful statement! In the end of the story, Job was able to bounce back and gained more than he had lost.

Have you ever gone through something in life which shook the very core of your existence? Have you ever lost something or someone who was very close to you? Have you experienced such a treacherous situation and you had no clue if and when you would make it through?

I was blessed to connect with a group of phenomenal women who have experienced different stories but had one thing in common, God brought them though some very dark places in life and they were able to overcome and so was I! My desire is as you read each of our stories, you are inspired and encouraged to hang on and know that out there in this world there is someone who has a similar experience and ultimately Bounced Back!

Chapter 1

What was I thinking?

By: Felicia C. Lucas

> For what shall it profit a man, if he shall gain the
> whole world, and lose his own soul? Mark 8:36

My husband and I have been married for twenty-one years, and a lot of people look at our pictures on social media and have commented, "They are so much in love," and yes, we had a fairy-tale beginning. We met in college, so you know; if there was a college newspaper headline it would say something like this, "College Grads Meet, They Fall in Love and Live Happily Ever After."

My husband graduated from North Carolina State University and I graduated from the University of North Carolina at Chapel Hill. And for those who know anything about college athletics, there is an intense rivalry between the NC State Wolfpack and the North

Carolina Tar Heels. Surprisingly, we are a house divided that gets along, very well.

We have been serving in ministry for the past 21 years together. I am a Pastor's Wife, the First Lady of the church. There are many pressures associated with being a first family. Many congregations put their pastors on pedestals, as if they can't experience any problems or have any challenges. Sometimes when the human side of being a pastor is exposed, many congregants find it hard to deal with it.

About nine years ago, I cheated on my husband and it wasn't with another man! It wasn't with another woman! I cheated on him with my job, which meant I put my job, I put my career above my marriage. So, I was having an inappropriate relationship with what I thought was the idea of success. We all know the traditional definition of cheating to be associated with infidelity in a sexual nature, but you can also cheat on your spouse with anything that you give more focus, more attention, more energy, more time, and more commitment to. And that's what I was doing. I was trying to climb the career ladder inappropriately. So, what does that look like? That means, every day I was

4

giving my job all of me and I had no balance. I was emotionally, physically, and mentally tied to my work.

For me, it was my job. But for you it could be something else. If you are in ministry, are you married to the church? Are you married to your children or other family members? Are you married to your friends? Are you married to the organizations that you're in, or to your sorority or fraternity? Anything that gets in the way of the commitment that you have with your spouse can create problems within the marriage.

Because of me spending time at work, I didn't know what was going on in my house. Since I was always working, it ended up that I was not going to Bible study or Sunday service. I also remember one incident, I chose to attend a sales meeting, and my husband had asked me to stop by the grocery store to pick up some items. I said I was not going to do it, and boy that was not the right answer.

That was one of the biggest arguments that we have ever had. I really felt like everything had come to a head by then. He was frustrated with me and in hindsight; I was so blind as to what was going on. In that moment, I thought that maybe I should just leave and not return home.

I was out building my business in an improper manner and that caused tremendous stress on my marriage. As a result, there was anger, resentment and frustration. A few days later, I was driving down the road and my husband called me on the phone and he said, "Do you want to be married?" The pastor called the First Lady and asked her did she want to be married? What in the world happened to us? We were at a very pivotal point in our marriage, and I had to decide as to what I wanted to do. It had to include a mindset shift and everything I deemed as important at the end of the day, wasn't important. It was important for me to go to my children's school and volunteer in the classroom. It was important for me to have the opportunity to go to their games. It was important for me to stay married, and that's when I realized I could lose it all.

The Bible says in Mark 8: 36, For what shall it profit a man, if he shall gain the whole world, and lose his own soul? I ask, what does it profit you to be the best coach? What does it profit you to be the best speaker? What does it profit you to be the expert in your field, if you gain all of that and you lose your family, or you lose who you are?

What do you do when your life is out of control and you need to bounce back?

I have four points using the letters in ***B.A.C.K:***

<u>**#1 BE HONEST**</u>: You must be honest about what happened. First, I had to be honest with God, because spending all that time at work and then all that extra time outside of work in building my entrepreneurial business, affected my relationship with God. Do you spend time with God and have a relationship with Him? Do you have intimacy with Him? I had to start there. I had to get it right with God! Second, I had to be honest to myself! What was I thinking? Lastly, I had to be honest with my husband. I know God put us together. I know we have purpose and a ministry assignment in the earth. I had to ask for forgiveness for what I caused to happen within our marriage and our household.

#2 ACKNOWLEDGE THE PROBLEM: The problem was with me, I had issues with time management. I was working in corporate, training leaders on time management and I was having a personal issue with time management and life balance. It is so funny that in life, that in which we struggle with is the area in which our ministry lies. I had to acknowledge that. I now manage my time better and I have a better life balance.

#3 CREATE INTIMACY AGAIN: In order to cultivate my relationship with God and my relationship with my husband, I have learned to use a very key word....NO! Sometimes when people ask me to do something that will take away from my time with God or the time with my family, I have to say no. So sometimes people ask me to do things at this point in my life, the answer is no. And it's ok for me to say, the answer is no, I'm not doing it. At this point in my life, I will not allow anything to jeopardize my relationship with God and with my husband and my children. So the answer is no. My husband and I have cultivated intimacy again in our marriage. God has opened many doors for us to travel and to explore the world. We do it because it helps us to stay connected.

#4 <u>KEEP GOD FIRST:</u> God is a jealous God. He doesn't want anything before Him. When you are bouncing back from life's blows and you are trying to figure out how do you go from this point in your life to the next phase of your life, you got to keep God first. I was not keeping God first and as a result, the stresses I was having, the anger I was having, the resentment I was feeling, all of these put stress in my marriage. My bounce back message is that God can restore and I am a living testimony!

DOWN FOR THE COUNT

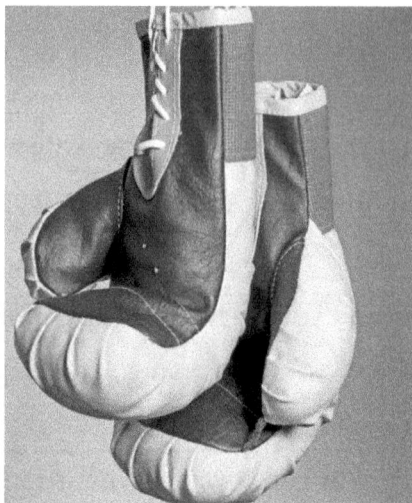

Chapter 2

From a Faceless Automaton to a Testimonial of God's Amazing Grace!

By: Christine Wilson

> **And be not conformed to this world: but be ye transformed by the renewing of your mind, that ye may prove what is that good, and acceptable, and perfect, will of God.**
>
> **Romans 12:2**

My story began with low self-esteem, insecurities, fears, and doubt. Let me tell you a brief story.

Several years ago, our Church Administrator asked me to read the Sunday morning announcements. Simple right? This is what fired in my head: *"WHAT! Oh my goodness. She can't be serious. She cannot be asking me to stand before the congregation, by myself, and DO ANYTHING! Absolutely not."* And for several weeks, I managed to get away with my "no," or so I thought.

About three Sundays later, our First Lady got nose to nose with me and said, "You can do this." Even while having that intense moment of fellowship with her, my head started hurting, my heart was pounding in my ears, the heat started rising from my collar, and I thought for sure I would pass completely out. Now you know the enemy was having a good time with that, right?

The next day on my way to intercessory prayer, God used that 45-minute ride to challenge me with the same question He asked Adam in the Garden of Eden: "Who told you, you were naked?" In essence, who told me I could not stand up and do something as simple as read the announcements? I had fallen prey to the wrong voice. But this didn't happen overnight. I had been collecting negative thoughts and statements for a very long time. This fortress of doubt and fears were almost a lifetime in the making.

In my arsenal of negative thoughts were statements like: "You're the spoiled child, the last of eleven, and will never amount to anything." "She's a bit chubby." "You should be more like this one or that one." My arsenal was so loaded with feelings of rejection and insecurities that even in my adult life when another lady in my presence would be complimented, it would necessarily cause my mind to think of rejection when there were no comments about me. Hearing **those statements** a time or two can only lead to self-doubt and a lack of confidence, which pushed me further into my shell.

So you see what happens when we entertain the wrong line of thinking or listen to the wrong voices? It can ruin your life for a very long time. Low self-esteem and insecurities wreaked such havoc in my life until it bled over into my marriage, opening the door to infidelity. It bled over into how I raised my children, how I performed on my jobs, and even how I functioned at church.

These insecurities turned into becoming a people-pleaser so much so that I felt like a hypocrite most of the time. I simply could not run the risk of people not liking or accepting me. Any amount of scrutiny would be factored into the equation of doubt and fears I constantly had playing in my head. I could not afford to have the scales I so carefully balanced to be toppled. So when I did come undone, you can only imagine the extremes. I could get so upset at the smallest things, and blow all the way up, simply because I had been holding so many other things down. When I lost my footing, the whole house of cards would fall.

Years before our Administrator pulled me out into the forefront; God was sending people into my world who spoke life to me. It was hard for me to believe because I had settled in and sat down under such a spirit of insecurity. I simply could not hear the voice God was using to speak life. That happens every time we give a place to the voice of the enemy. We sit down under the oppression; we settle into a place of lifelessness. We take ownership of it, which brings a halt to the plans and purposes of God being carried out in our lives.

June 10, 2013 was a pivotal day for me. I was rushed into emergency surgery to remove a liter of fluid from around my heart! That started me on a spiritual quest beginning with tearing down the walls of insecurity and fear. These walls locked me in such a tight space until it became hard to breathe. The irony was my physical state of being was a direct replica of my spiritual state of being; I simply could no longer breathe. Since the surgery, I have come to grips with my "why" and in the process; I found writing brings me life and great joy. This new life I am discovering is wonderful and the process of transformation has been captivating.

When I started writing the weekly inspirations for our church bulletin, I never could have imagined the journey it would take me on. I was a timid, insecure, frightened, introvert who didn't think she had anything to say or add to any discussion. I wore so many masks until I didn't even know who I was. I made it my mission to find out how others expected me to be and worked diligently to be that person. Mind you, most of the unsubstantiated criteria was stuff I had running through my own mind. Very few people actually took advantage of my blatant lack of confidence.

One of the dynamics to bouncing back is how God can bring you through such an ordeal and deposit you into your new normal so smoothly and seamlessly that sometimes it's even hard to believe you once felt that way, or believed like that, or did those things. It's our amazing Father's love for us that will wipe away the sting of even ***that*** death in our lives.

Through this great metamorphosis, I am now being charged with letting others know that God has need of you. Just as He trusted me with everything I went through, God has trusted you with the nuances of your journey, too. God knew Job and what he would do when the enemy went several rounds with him; God also knew what you would do when faced with the obstacles in your life. For me, praise is what I do, and that is exactly what I did throughout each and every hardship I faced. I went to God and we reasoned together. Even though the situation did not change immediately, I went back to my posture of praise and thanksgiving. Even while working through the doubt, fears, and low self-esteem, I always found my place of peace and strength in prayer, praise, and worship.

Rejection is real. Feelings of inadequacy are real. But these feelings will cause us not to agree with God and who He has created us to be. These emotions will cause us not to shine, and that is what He is doing in this hour of Christendom... bringing us into the spotlight to shine for Him. So I encourage anyone who is good and tired of being a people-pleaser to simply start by agreeing with God that you are fearfully and wonderfully made. Get into the Word and receive all the love God wants to pour out on you as you look to Him and realize He didn't make anything that's not good and that includes you.

Stop pushing pause and putting your life on hold waiting for others to approve and validate you. God has already approved us and appointed us for right now, filled with purpose. He is the final authority on you and on me. His Word spoken over us has to be received and applied or otherwise, we will never get over being people-pleasers.

Don't dim your light because others don't see you for who you were created to be. Believe God really will use you, because He can and He will. Don't shrink back, because we need you in full throttle being all God created you to be. He gave you the assignment you're walking in right now. Get in line with God and watch Him open doors for you and set you on the street called straight, bringing you right into your purpose. The only person in your way now is you.

After emergency surgery, I was forced to look at my life from a different perspective. Overly concerned about the opinions of others had to take second and third place; God has gotten my attention now. He wants to know what I have done with what He deposited within me. He has that same question for you. What are you doing with what He deposited within you? How are you displaying His grace and glory to a world desperately in need of someone to step outside the box and be authentic? You will never please all of the people all of the time, or even most of the people some of the time, but you can please God with your "Yes" to His will for your life. Be brave enough to say "Yes," and watch Him take you places you never thought you would go; do things you never thought you would do; and say things you didn't even know you knew to say to effectuate change in someone else's life. I was down for the count, but I bounced back – so can you. I believe in you.

Chapter 3

Knocked Down but
Not Knocked Out

By: Detra Williams

> **God is our refuge and strength, a very present
> help in trouble. Psalms 46:1**

The count begins; the earthly referee begins to count,
"1, 2, 3, 4, 5, 6, 7, 8, 9, 10, you're out!" The count
begins; the heavenly referee begins to count, "10, 9, 8,
7,6,5,4,3,2,1, you're in." I cannot count how many
times I was knocked down and counted out. My life
started with me being a happy well-rounded little girl,
most people will tell you that I was a tomboy. I would
run and jump around with the best of them. I would
climb trees, play football, and out-run any man, boy, or
child in the neighborhood. There was nothing a boy
could do that I could not do better. I was one of those
girls.

If you looked at my family from the outside, you would think that we were the model family. We lived in a middle-class neighborhood; our family was the fourth black family, but the second black family with children. There was not a lot to do because most of the white children were not allowed to play with us, but we still had fun with the kids we could play with. As children, we did not understand that this was racism; and honestly, it did not matter to us, we found ways to play with some of the white children. We had a Mom and Dad in the home that both worked. There was also my grandmother that lived in the home as well, she also worked part-time cleaning houses; but she was always there when we got home from school. But behind closed doors there was a different story; we lived in pure HELL.

We walked on eggshells. We never knew what type of mood my father would be in when he came home. My father was an alcoholic and an abuser. He would beat my Mom with broom handles, butt of a gun, his fist or, whatever else he could find. Although he would send us outside, most of the time, we could still hear what was going on, and we of course, could see the results of the beating when we saw our mother. If that wasn't enough, at the age of six, my Uncle came to live with us and he was so much fun, he was a big kid at heart. He would spend a lot of time with us, playing inside and outside of the house. However, a year later, things begin to change. My Mom got a job where she worked late; so she was not home, my Dad would be sleep, or out drinking. Grandma would be in her room sleep.

At night, my Uncle would enter my bedroom, he would shake my feet to wake me up, and all I could see was that shadow waving at me to follow him. Not knowing any better, I did just that, I got out of bed and followed him. Well, at first there was a lot of fondling, that dark figure would rub my flat chest in which I had no breast (but it was satisfying to him), and then he would begin to move his hand down in my pajamas and rub my vagina. He would put his finger inside me and it would hurt, but he would always say relax. He would have his finger inside my vagina while rubbing his penis at the same time. I'm just lying there crying and thinking: Why? He would stop when that "white stuff" would come out of the head of his penis. I didn't know what it was; I only knew when he did that, it means he was going to stop. This went on for years. I never said a word to anyone, and no one ever noticed anything. I just knew that someone would see something different in me, or they could just tell. As a child, it was hard for me to believe that no one knew what was going on. Can they tell by the way I walk that something was different? Can they tell by the way I was acting and being defiant? (I have never been this way before). Someone should see something different in me and tell something was wrong with me.

One day, my Uncle and I were home alone (not sure why) and I felt safe because nothing ever happened during the daytime. So, I was good, sitting watching TV, and during the commercials I would play bob jacks. But he approached me and grabbed my hand and led me to the garage (this is where he took me each time he molested me). He laid me down on the floor, and the pain was worse than ever before. As he attempted to rape me; he realized that it was not going to be easy. See, I was still a virgin, and no one or nothing had ever entered that perfect spot except his finger; his penis would not go in. As he continued to proceed in his gratification, he was still having a difficult time. He decided to spit on my vagina, so it would become moist so that he could complete his mission. This went on for a few months, then I started my period and he would not touch me. I prayed that my period would stay on forever.

Well at the age of 12, I became pregnant, and without saying a word, my parents agreed that I would get an abortion. I had no voice, nor did I want to. Although I wasn't a liar, considering I was a child, I felt that no one would believe me. He did not go to trial, when he went to see his lawyer, my Grandmother went with him and that is when she found out that I was a victim. All she asked me was, why didn't I tell her? She never spoke another word about it. My molester took a plea deal because I wasn't the only one he had molested. He was sentenced to 25 years to life due to prior criminal convictions. Like most young girls molested, I became promiscuous, and throughout my life, I have looked for love in all the wrong places.

At the age of 19, I met and married a preacher and I just knew my life was turning around. I knew finally I have found love and I was going to be happy. Well, the happiness did not last long; a few months after we married, the true man came out. He pulled off the wolf in sheep's clothing and became like any other man. He began to cheat and later, I found out that he had slept with so many women in and outside of the church. I gave birth to a handsome baby boy and a year later divorced him. Then there was another, then another man, still looking for love in ALL OF THE WRONG PLACES.

Until one day, I met the real man of my life (at least I thought so). This man treated me like no other; he would buy me stuff, walk me to the bus stop and sometimes ride with me. See I was a simple woman, so I did not need for you to spend a million dollars on me. All I really wanted was for someone to spend personal time with me, love me, touch me, and be good to me. He started out that way. He was great to my son and to me. The first time he hit me, should have been the last time. I was naive and thought he was smoking cigarettes, but later found out that he was smoking marijuana and crack. I confronted him one day and he slapped me so hard that I got dizzy. But I still stayed because he said that he loved me, and he would never do it again. You know that did not last long. He went from slapping me to kicking, hitting, punching, and finally raping me numerous times. He would beat me and then want to have sex, and of course I did not want to, but I did not have a choice because he said that my body belonged to him, and he will take what he wanted. After a while I would just have sex with him because if I didn't, he would take it, the pain was so bad. He would do vaginal and anal which was the worse, but I had no choice because again my body was not my body, according to him.

One time he attempted to brand his initials on the inside of my thighs with a wire coat hanger that he had put on the stove to get hot (but I fought him this time and WON). He fractured my right arm because I would not give him oral sex. There were times he would smoke crack and could not get an erection and blamed me for it and he would beat me. I would get punched in the mouth when I talked back, he fractured my nose because I did not get paid one Friday, but he forgot that I did not work the week before because he had fractured my right arm and I couldn't type (that is what I did at work). I attempted suicide and he beat me after one attempt because I didn't do it right. Then another time I attempted suicide and we were riding in the ambulance and he leaned over to tell me, if I don't die he would kill me later. Well, I didn't die but I still went back, for more pain. But what was I supposed to do? I felt like I was nothing, he made me feel like I was nothing. My mind was so twisted, I felt that I was getting everything I deserve and that one day maybe he would finally kill me and put me out of my misery. Each beating I would pray that it was the last, that this time he will hit me so hard that I would lose conscious and die. My wish never came true, after each hit, I would still get up.

I felt that this was going to be how I would spend the rest of my life. I spent eight years with this man who said that he would love me to death. I did not realize that he literally meant to death. Through all the beatings, I had given birth to a handsome baby boy; we had two sons and he was a good father, but an awful husband. God had opened the door many times for me to leave but only to return. I had three miscarriages due to the beatings, attempted suicide three times to just get away from the beatings, but did not know what I was doing so as you can tell I was not successful.

My life flashed before my eyes once again, this beating was the worst and this is the only time I knew this was the end. I had knots upside my head, busted lips, black eyes, and he would have killed me if I had not run. I ran for my life and never looked back. He was arrested a few days later and diagnosed with bipolar and a personality disorder. Again, I left and never looked back, and that was in 1995 and I have not seen him in person since I left. He sent me a friend request on Facebook and of course I deleted the request quickly.

This bounce back process was not easy. My life began to make a turn for the better. I met a man over the phone; we dated long distance until I finally moved to North Carolina in July 1997. My Children came to live with us in North Carolina in July 1999. I had lived in fear for so long and I just knew over time that this man would beat me too. We did not have a perfect marriage, but he allowed me to be me and I appreciate that more than anything. I never knew who I was before 1999, but I knew I wanted more out of life than to walk around in fear and wondering: What If? In my women support groups, I would hear people say to surround yourself with positive, like-minded people. I did just that, I surrounded myself with positive people,

people who wanted the best out of life. Not to live life the same as the year before. Still this was not easy, but through determination, encouragement from others, and finally being healed from my past life through forgiveness, true healing, and deliverance; I finally realized that I am a strong, independent, Servant of the almighty God, and I am a queen in His kingdom. There were times that I hated and blamed God for everything I was going through, but without God being by my side every step of the way, I would be dead by now.

I dealt with depression, post-traumatic stress, and was put on medication. I finally knew what it felt like to be loved and to have a life. I was able to graduate from college at the age of 47 with my Bachelor's Degree in Social Work and graduated at the age of 50 with my Master's Degree. I am an ordained Minister, motivational speaker, author, mother, and grandmother.

But my life changed on November 18, 2017, as I was away speaking at a Domestic Violence event, God whispered into my husband's ear and took him home to be with Him and this was a blow to my spirit because he was a great supporter of my Ministry. Although he never read one word of my writing, he only knew what I told him, and he said that was enough. After his death, within one week of his funeral, my father passed away.

Here I was again, preparing for yet another funeral, saying another final good-bye to yet another important man in my life. I felt like giving up, this is too much for one person to handle. I still have not had the chance to grieve for my sister who passed away in December 2015 because I had to be there for everyone. Still to this day, I still have not been able to truly grieve for the two most important men in my life that died much too soon. But I knew I couldn't give up, I knew I had a story to tell and I know these men, although no longer physically here on earth, would not want me to give up. I knew their spirit was pushing me to keep going.

At my husband's funeral, my cousin whispered in my ear, "God made you for a time such as this." I had no clue what he meant until my father's death. God had destined me for greatness before I was formed in my mother's womb, and although I may feel that I had a rough life, look at me now. Most people would have been successful in their attempted suicides, but God knew His plans for my life. God has given me so many opportunities to share my story, and I want to encourage others that they can overcome anything if you have God on your side. I had people praying for me until I was able to pray for myself. Each time I speak of my past life, I gain strength which allows me to continue to share my story. I am no longer ashamed of my past; my past does not define my future. I may have been knocked down, I may have been counted out, but God picked me up and counted me in.

Chapter 4

Blinded by Love

By: Nichole Bobbitt

> **To give them beauty for ashes, the oil of joy for mourning, the garment of praise for the spirit of heaviness: Isaiah 61:3**

I was seventeen; he was twenty-one when we met at a club. His name was Donald. After we dated for a while, I was in love with him; he was the first real relationship I ever had. Donald was charming, giving me things, taking me places. I lived in the country and never went anywhere, so when he took me out, I loved it. I was still in high school, but every weekend he would pick me up. It was good until Baby Mama started causing us trouble; yes he had two kids already. One night we went out and Baby Mama showed up, and Donald jumped on her, and I was shocked, and I was like he wouldn't do that to me. The Baby Mama, Angela was screaming and fighting back, but she was determined to ride with us. Although Angela was causing the problem, I was thinking how can Donald do that; and will he do that to me? After we finally left, I was shocked and amazed for the rest of the night and scared to upset him.

One evening, Donald came over and I was across the street when he came over, so he sent my brother to get me. When I arrived home, we began to argue, and I talked back, so next thing I knew, my lip was bleeding from him hitting me. On another day, Donald came over in the middle of the night because I had gone out, so he started fussing and ended up hitting me like a man. I fell into my bedroom closet. I was screaming and crying and some friends were at my house and no one helped me. I was mad at them for a while because they didn't help. Those were the first time of many hits from him. Throughout the years, there was slapping, punching, chasing me, kicking me, throwing drinks in my face. I would go out if he was at work, he would come get me from the club and fight me. When he showed up at the club, I was scared so I just left to keep from being embarrassed in front of people. Even when he was the one screwing up our relationship, he still hit me. He was the one cheating, I catch him, but he wants to fight me. I started feeling unwanted and not loved, and too embarrassed to tell someone.

As a woman being hit by the man who claims to love you make you feel very low and unwanted, scared, and surely not loved. Sometimes your mind gets to thinking crazy things. I started praying and asking God to help me get the courage to leave and make it on my own. I was working part-time at the time and receiving public assistance. But after praying, I got a full-time job and the nerve to finally say, "Get out of my house fool." The day I finally told him to get out, he wanted to act so loving to me, but I stood strong and kept to my word. He left after a week and he kept calling and coming by for a few weeks. But I didn't fall for it. I had been asking God to send me that man who is loving and caring who would not ever hit me.

After a few years of waiting, God sent him to me. This man is so wonderful, he is loving, caring, he makes me laugh, he holds me tight, and he cares about me. He teaches me about things I don't know. He is very mature. He doesn't hit me and he doesn't even argue with me, he walks off if we have a disagreement. As a beautiful creation of God, a woman shouldn't have to be abused. We are to be loved. Being hit is not love, I learned the hard way. To my ladies and especially young ladies, you don't have to let a man beat on you, thinking he loves you, that's not love. You can find true love. I did!

My Poem

Through it all,

I built a wall.

With all the pain,

I thought I was going insane.

So I stayed behind this wall,

and hoping it won't fall.

The walls kept me safe.

With the Lord's Mercy and Grace.

When prayers go up, blessings come down

Chapter 5

I am a Living Testimony

By: Diane Pace

> **And the peace of God, which surpasses all understanding will guard your hearts and minds through Christ Jesus. Philippians 4:7**

When I think of the goodness of Jesus, and all He has done for Diane, my soul cries out Hallelujah. I thank God for saving me. Thank God for second chances. I thank Him for the many times that He has spared my life from seen and unseen dangers. I've seen many near death experiences during my lifetime, but none of them can compare to the one on September 14, 2014, at approximately 2:38 a.m., when I almost died. I was down or the count, but God said, not so.

On Saturday night, September 13, 2014, I went to bed feeling healthy like any other night. I wasn't feeling sick and I hadn't done anything out of the norm. Later during the night, I awake from a deep sleep to use the restroom. While in the restroom, I began to feel sick. I felt nauseated, then I felt like I was about to pass out. I was thinking, Lord what in the world? I had all types of thoughts racing through my head. On this particular night, my husband Raymond never heard me get up. So I was thinking if I pass out in the restroom, he won't know it. I thought if I could at least make it back to the bed, I would be alright. I managed to make it to the bed but couldn't get on the bed. Our bed sits high and I didn't have the strength to climb in bed. I couldn't call out to Raymond. All I was able to do was lie down on the floor alongside the bed to keep from falling. In the midst of trying to lie down to keep from falling, I felt the strange need to know the time. The digital clock on my nightstand had 2:38 a.m.

As I lie there on the floor, I began to get cold. I felt my body began to shut down. It felt like there was a decrease in my blood circulation. Then it seems like my vital organs, were stopping. During this time, I heard my husband say, "Di, what are you doing on the floor?" I couldn't move, and I couldn't respond. Meanwhile, I was still just lying there helpless. While lying there, I knew I was actually dying. Next, I felt when my bowel muscles relaxed. I felt the coldness flow down my legs and to my feet. It felt like someone had poured ice water in my bloodstream. Then in an instant I could feel my body functioning as normal. I felt my blood circulating like normal again. My body warmed up and I was able to move and speak. I was down for the count, but God said, not so. Hallelujah! To God be all the glory! I began to pray and thank God for my life. I knew He had spared me for a reason. I slowly got off the floor and got in bed. I didn't tell Raymond right then. I didn't want to frighten my husband and have him staring at me for the rest of the night. Later that morning, I began to explain to him why I was on the floor.

That afternoon, I had called and explained everything to my daughter, Renee. I told Renee, God knew I had some works that were left undone. I began to discuss some matters with Renee that needed to be handled in the event of untimely demise. Later that day, I was telling a friend about my experience. They laughed and asked, "Why did you need to know what time it was, had you died who were you going to tell?" I laughed and said, "I don't know, I just know at the time it was relevant." Now I know why the time was relevant. God knew what He was doing. He spared me and I'm able to tell my story. I was so close to death, I began to wonder, why did God spare my life? Maybe He did it to get my attention. All I know is I began to take inventory of my life. Was I headed to heaven or hell?

Prior to that date, I thought nothing could separate me from the love of God. (Romans 8:38, 39) For I am persuaded, that neither death, nor life, nor angels, nor principalities, nor powers, nor things present, nor things to come, nor height, nor depth, nor any other creature shall be able to separate us from the love of God, which is in Christ Jesus our Lord. I was living righteous and serving God. I was studying the Word. I was humble. I would pray and ask God to forgive my transgressions. I would even ask Him to forgive those that trespassed against me. (Mark 11:25) And whenever you stand praying, forgive if you have anything against anyone, so that your Father also who is in heaven may forgive you your trespasses." As I began to examine myself, I began to ask: Had I died? Is there anything at all that would have separated me from God? While processing these thoughts, I began to realize just how easy I had let my guard down. (1 Peter 5:8-9).

We must be sober-minded and watchful. Satan is always on the prowl, waiting for an opportunity for a crack to slip in. To let down our guard against sin for even a moment gives him the moment he has been waiting for. His whole desire is to turn us from God. If we are watching and praying, then we can always resist him, firm in our faith, knowing that the same kinds of suffering are being experienced by our brotherhood throughout the world. While I was pondering on rather I was living my very best as a Christian, I thought of the seven churches in the Book of Revelation. I thought about how the seven churches had fallen short. The Apostle John received a revelation from Jesus Christ which is what we now call the Book of Revelation. In this vision, Christ gave John seven messages for seven first-century churches in Asia Minor. Christ explained to each church what they've done correctly and their shortcomings. I begin to reflect on so many things.

While I was searching my heart, I asked myself: What are my shortcomings? Have I truly forgiven people? Had I died that night, what would God have told me about Diane? Have I forgiven family, friends, ex coworkers, or even my enemies? Have I forgiven the loved one that attacked my character? Have I forgiven the person that lied on me? Have I forgiven my debtors? What about the people that deliberately never paid what they owed me? What about the people that always made excuses to keep from paying their bail debts? Yet, I allowed them to be free because of the God in me. Many times I would go out of my way to help someone because they asked. Yet they would always bite the hand that fed them. Had I forgiven those people? Was there any malice I was harboring in my heart for those people?

John 10:10 states, "The thief comes only to steal and kill and destroy. I came that they may have life and have it abundantly. "This Scripture is not talking about nor limited to material things. The enemy will steal your joy, kill your peace, and destroy your relationship with God if you're not watchful. (Galatians 5:22, 23) states, "But the fruit of the Spirit is love, joy, peace, patience, kindness, goodness , faithfulness, gentleness, self-control; against such things there is no law. On that day, I realized that I do not love anyone that good that I'm going to hell because of who they are. I began to pray like Jesus. Luke 23:34 saying "Father, forgive them for they know not what they do." I began to pray for them like I've never prayed before. I began to forgive the unpaid debts and clean the slate with a zero balance. God gave me peace with those that had taken advantage of my kindness.

I bounced back and every day is a new opportunity for a closer walk with God. I learned that what I thought was my best wasn't good enough. I've faithfully worked on letting stuff go; no matter how much it hurts. When I forgive, I have peace that only God can give. (Philippians 4:7) and the peace of God, which surpasses all understanding, will guard your hearts and minds through Christ Jesus. Now I'm very careful not to allow the snares of the enemy separate me from the love of God. God is my protector. No weapon that is formed against me shall prosper. He reminded me of 1 Chronicles 16:21, He suffered no man to do them wrong: yea, he reproved kings for their sakes, saying, Touch not mine anointed, and do my prophets no harm. I have truly included forgiveness for others in my everyday walk. With that forgiveness, I continue to have my peace.

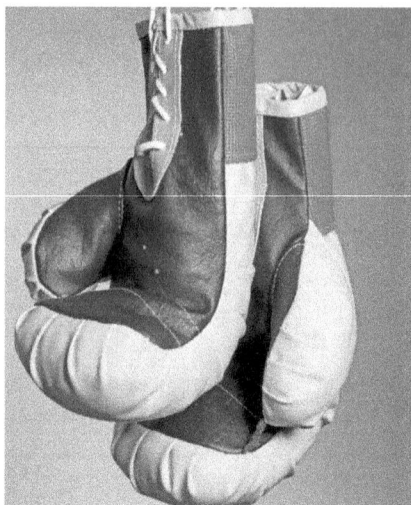

Chapter 6

My Soul Looks Back and Wonders How I Got Over

By: Pamela Carroll

> **The Lord is my light and my Salvation; whom shall I fear? The Lord is the strength of my life; of whom shall I be afraid Psalm 27:1**

Locked in the bedroom of our military housing, the lights turned off at the breaker box in the utility room. On the other side of our bedroom door, I hear the voice of my husband. He is slowly saying, "I am the devil, let me in. "I am frightful and crying from the fear of the darkness and what is on the other side of the door. What started off as being playful, seems to turn out to be a sign from God.

At the age of twenty-two, I fell head over heels for an infantry soldier; I met when I arrived at Fort Benning, Georgia, serving in the Army. We were married for four years and had three children. The darkness came with the announcement of deployment to Desert Storm. We said our good-byes in the airplane hangar. I remember all the other families and the soldier's loved ones hugging and crying. I did not cry. I was a soldier and a soldier's wife. I'm a trooper. I can do this. All the soldiers direct themselves to formation to board the plane. I quickly drive down the road to pull over to the side to watch the plane take off. The other wives and I stood quietly as the plane took off in full speed down the runway. As the wheels left the pavement, my heart fell to the ground. I fell on emptiness, realizing he is gone.

Six months went by of adjusting to marriage and then becoming a single mother to our son. My husband is home. The physical changes were obvious. He had been injured when his mortar tract jumped a ditch and he fell back and fractured his tailbone. The mental changes took a while for me to put my finger on it, but I did notice that he was a little withdrawn. I sat him down to discuss with him about counseling, but he never went. As soon as he returned, we were part of the baby boomers. We had a daughter.

As time went by, things never got any better. Going through depression, I decided not to stay in the army and became a full-time housewife. When we used to be together, all of the time turned into I'm home alone most of the time with the kids. He would hang out with his buddy's a lot; and his drinking increased. I did not recognize the man I was living with, but I continued to keep our family together and work on our marriage. He got out of the army and we moved to Missouri. We initially stayed at his best friend's home until we both got jobs and got our own home.

I noticed that things were still the same. He was gone the entire weekend. As soon as he returned, I confronted him that I was not going through this same mess again. We argued, but I did not back down before I got pushed against the wall. I don't remember where I got it from, but before I knew it, I had a gun in my hands, aiming to shoot. Before I can disengage the safety button, I feel a great blow on the side of my head. I was hit so hard, the earring stud I was wearing was missing. We had always argued, but that was the first time that he hit me; and it was not the last. After that moment, I lived in hell. I lived in a place where I didn't have friends and just knew his family. All I had was my son and daughter. He continued to provide for us, he got us a home; but still a lot of times he was not home.

I had got a job at a nursing home as a Certified Nursing Assistance. When I would call home from work, a woman would answer my phone. I had never known anyone to experience what I had just gone through, but his sister tells me that I needed to accept it because that is how the men in her family acted. I really did not know what to do next, but I just continued to take care of my kids. Fighting her did not make me feel any better. I don't know what was going through my mind. I just knew I always did the best I could and made all others happy. But I was not happy. I didn't want to be in this world anymore. When I went to bed, I did not want to wake up.

The only thing I could find in the house was a bottle of Benadryl. I took the contents of the bottle of about twenty pills and went to sleep. But I woke up sick; throwing up all that was in my stomach. At that moment, I did something I believe was my first time, because I don't remember ever doing this before. I talked to God and I felt that I was kept there for a reason. I didn't know what reason, but it wasn't my time to leave.

It was not easy. But I utilized my army training mentality and would tell myself that I am a soldier, just keep marching forward. I was living far from my parents, and my sister was stationed in Germany. They had no clue of how I was living. I felt alone. He continued to see this woman and eventually stopped coming home. But still I continued to try to save my marriage and focused on taking care of my children. All I had was my job, but it didn't pay enough. Just paying the rent, electricity, and buying food was difficult to maintain.

I began to go to the plasma center to get fifteen dollars to buy diapers and a bag of beans and rice for us to eat. I just did the best I could trying to survive. And the little bit I did have to get ahead; he would come and beat me up and take my money. The last fight we had, I was hit so hard, I could not open my mouth. I thought I had a broken jaw. I decided then that I needed to get away.

After being chased around town with the kids in the car, I ended up at a women's shelter. As soon as the time came, my kids and I were on a bus headed to North Carolina to my parent's home. I was ordered to return to Missouri to answer to charges of kidnapping of the children, because I crossed state lines without the consent of the other parent. He was able to become the primary custodian of the kids. I felt like I had lost everything. But I was blessed with something that gave me strength to keep going on. I found out I was with child with a son. My plan was to work and keep in contact with my kids.

I had to make a difficult decision to move to North Carolina. But with the help of my parents, I had a place to call home when I arrived there with all I could fit in the car. I just worked on improving myself and making sure we would never be hungry or homeless again. I carried a hole in my heart because my kids were separated. But we were able to be parents that could work together for the sake of the kids. They would alternate their school and summer visits. I did all I could do to keep them together. I was able to get a great job working with adults that are mentally challenged. I did get married again.

Unfortunately, the second husband of eight years put me back where I had started from, but that's another story to be told. God did place someone on my

48

path that became my third husband that I had to learn to express love that I had buried deep down inside. I had to work on me. I had to forgive and let go. Without my past, I would not be who I am today. I continue to use my experiences to encourage others that they do not have to stay in the darkness. God gives us the strength to get back up and keep marching on. Giving up is not an option, I survived what I was placed into and it made my faith stronger. I am no longer that scared woman crying behind a door in a dark room. I found that light that I have been searching for. I am a fighter and the most satisfying victory was becoming a soldier in the Army of our Lord and Savior.

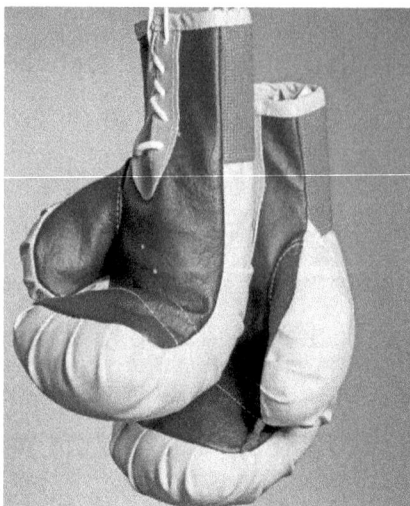

Chapter 7

From Pain to Purpose

By: Shonte Monroe

She is clothed with strength and dignity
Proverbs 31: 25

Welcome to my world! I started out as a young girl taking care of two sick parents. My father is still living; however, my mother died September, 2010. In my life there have been some defining moments. Moments I thought I was going to collapse, but the grace of God kept me!!!

As I begin this writing journey, I begin to think about so many life lessons and testimonies that I have. I can truly say I have had a rough life, but God has been so good to me. During my thought process, I prayed and asked God should I share about Fear trying to take me out on several occasions. Should I share about the many failed relationships to the point of me almost losing hope? Should I share about the many levels of church hurt that bruised me deeply in my past? Or should I tell them about getting married at an early age only to be divorced in six months which turned from shame to shine! Should I tell them about having a rough childhood and having my identity zapped from me because at times I didn't know who I was?! My life hasn't always been perfect, but it's definitely been worth it.

As I begin to reflect on my life, a Scripture comes to mind, I will praise you because I am fearfully and wonderfully made, your works are wonderful, I know full well. Psalms 139:14. So let's dig a little deeper and discover the past -present- future.

So here we go! Let's dive in! As a young girl, age nine, to be exact; me and my father was in a critical accident which caused him to become paralyzed and I was in the truck with him, I walked away with no scratches on me. Thank God, I am not hurt at all from the accident, just bad memories. So as you know, that changed my life forever.

Years later, my mom was diagnosed with kidney failure. Jesus be a fence now, I have two sick parents. I was hurt and crushed thinking why me? What have I done to have sick parents?! I went through a lot during that process. But all along, God had a plan and He was developing me into my purpose. You see, at the time, I didn't understand, but now I see what the fight was all about. I basically had to grow up really fast....

Now one thing is for sure, I learned the name Jesus at an early age! There is definitely power in that name. That name got me through the storm! The name above all names! I get excited just thinking about that name! Oh how I love Jesus! I'm having a moment, please excuse me! It's just so sweet to know Him and how He has made so many ways even in tough times.

As I begin to grow up, I had an identity crisis because of all the things that happened to me in my childhood. I found myself getting in relationships because of those three famous words, "I love you." Sadly to say, I was in two abusive relationships, but I got out of both safely. God is a keeper. Then as I got a little older, I lost my mom at the age of 23, a very tough time of my life. The growing pains were real. Then a little after that, I felt like running away from all of my problems, so I decided to get married all for the wrong reasons. I was only married for six months. Needless to say, I got a divorce. The word divorce tried to destroy me. During that time, my name was slandered all over the place. I lost many friends. I was embarrassed and ashamed. People were laughing and pointing their fingers at me. I got told I would never be anything or anybody special.

I'm so glad the devil is a **Big** liar. After that process, I went through the pruning stage. God shaped me, molded me, gave me a new name, and everything. I devoted my time to serving God wholeheartedly and building my relationship with Him on a personal level. I learned to put my trust in God 100% no matter what. I began to reach goals that I had always dreamed of.

Two years later, I became an author, motivational speaker, and CEO of the Cupcakes and Conversations Movement. My life had improved tremendously. God had done a mighty work. Everything I had dreamed about came to past. I'm so thankful that I didn't listen to the naysayers and dream killers.

So, then I experienced the thing that cut me the most, Church Hurt; something that most people don't like to deal with nor talk about. It happens every day. Well I learned after going through it several times, it's not the actual church that hurt you, but it's the mean-spirited people. God is love. God doesn't hurt us. He loves us and is concerned about us. My experiences in church got worse at times to the point where I said, "You know what? Forget it. I'm not going to anybody's church." That was the devil. Now keep in the mind, the devil is after the Word of God. He doesn't want you to get the Word. Because when you get the Word and apply to your life, you are a bad somebody! So that's what he is after.

I am happy to say that I have found the right place for me because sometimes we can be in the wrong place. It's okay to discover that you are not where you should be! Pray and ask God to lead you. So after all I have been through in a church setting, I have vowed to God and said that ain't no devil in hell running me from my set place. I am free and I will continue to stay free and walk in love. I am determined to love the unlovable. I am a true storm survivor because not only did I survive my life issues; but I overcame big obstacles that was determined to take me out.

Always remember, it's not how you start, but how you finish. I'm so happy at this moment in my life. I can truly say I'm living the best life. My lesson for this story is; follow God no matter what; and you will never go wrong. Never listen to dream killers, keep your eyes on the prize. Follow your heart and dreams. Stay focused. It's never too late to start over. I did it, and so can you. Be encouraged, always remember: Life is Challenging, but Hang in There!

About the Authors

Visionary Author, Felicia C. Lucas

Felicia Lucas is a #1 International Best-Selling Author and 3 Time Best Selling Author, Speaker, Empowerment Coach and Book Publisher. Minister Felicia and her husband, Pastor Kelvin Lucas, co-founded *Take It By Force Ministries*, Inc. a non-profit youth and young adult 501©3 organization and *Dominion Tabernacle Church*. They were married in 1997 and have three children. As a business woman on the move, she is the CEO of *His Glory Creations Publishing LLC*. His Glory Creations Publishing, LLC is a Christian book publishing house which provides self-publishing services for clients. They help launch and scale the creative works of new, aspiring and seasoned authors across the globe, through stories that are inspirational, empowering, life-changing or educational in nature, including fiction and non-fiction.

She is the 2016 Recipient of the NC Career Woman of the Year Award by the NC Business and Professional Women Club. Felicia graduated from the University of North Carolina at Chapel Hill with a BA Degree in Speech Communications. For over twenty years, she has worked in the human resources field.

Other published book projects and titles by Felicia include:

- ***Make it Happen: Moving Towards Your Best U!***
- ***Get in the Game: A Teen's Playbook for Winning the Game of Life***
- ***The Bounce Back: Triumphant Stories of Resiliency and Perseverance***
- ***Stuff: A Collection of Creative Middle School Short Stories, Volumes 1 and 2***

AUTHOR CHRISTINE WILSON

For more than 25 years, Christine has been an encourager and an exhorter, so it was easy to now find her flow in inspirational writing. In 2017 she became a published author of *Authentically You*. She is the founder of Scribe4Him Publishing to help others get their books out to the world.

You can discover her at her Mid-Week Motivation live-stream on Facebook, where she inspires others to follow their God-given paths. Her desire is to motivate and fan the flame that was ignited in you on the day of your birth.

In July 2016 Christine received the E.K. Bailey Expository Preacher's Certificate at the annual Conference in Dallas, Texas. She and her husband,

Andy, have been married 29 years, live in Germantown, Maryland, have three children, and 13 grandchildren. More than anything, it is her desire to see you live your very best life worshipping God and serving others.

AUTHOR DETRA WILLIAMS

And we know that all things work together for good to them that love God, to them who are the called according to his purpose (Romans 8:28 KJV).

Detra Denise Williams is a mother, grandmother and a recent widow who currently works in Child Protective Service as a Forensic Social Worker at her Local Government Agency. Detra Williams is also a co-author, and an ordained minister, which earned her the title of an Evangelist.

Being physically, sexually, emotionally, and financially abused can have a lifelong effect and can determine your overall outcome in life. She hopes that sharing her story can be a source of courage and strength to anyone that she encounters. She hopes to empower and encourage those victims that they too can face and conquer the challenges and be a proud survivor of Domestic Violence.

AUTHOR NICHOLE BOBBITT

Nichole Bobbitt was born as Nichole Lee in a little town called Pleasant Hill NC. She is the oldest of her mother's six children. Nichole is the mother of three boys and is raising her nephew & one granddaughter. Nichole works as a security guard and takes classes online at her local community college. Nichole has a vision to help young ladies and desires to open her own book store and lounge one day.

AUTHOR DIANE PACE

Diane Pace was born in Smithfield, NC and now resides in Wendell, NC. Diane is the daughter of the late Willie Harvey Turner II and Frances Turner. Through that union she is the youngest of seven siblings. She is a loving wife to her husband Raymond Pace. She is a mother of six children. She has nine grandchildren and one great grandchild. Diane is the mother hen to many of her children's friends, her cousins, her nieces and her nephews.

She is the owner of Pace Bail Bonding and a Minister at Delightful Temple Ministries in Kenly, NC under the leadership of Pastor Joe McDougald and his wife Co Pastor Justeen McDougald.

AUTHOR PAMELA CARROLL

Pamela was born in Durham, North Carolina. She is a wife, mother, sister and grandmother and has served in the United States Army. She loves to help others and knows that she has a gift and the patience of a caregiver. She has the most rewarding job of working with individuals that are mentally and physically challenged. She ensures that they have the simple things of life that most take for granted. But fairness, respect and dignity of life tops them all. She is 51 years old and has recently answered the call into ministry and is ready for what God wants her to do. She thanks God for preparing her to open her mouth to share her story.

AUTHOR SHONTE MONROE

Shonte Monique Monroe is a native of North Carolina. She works in the health care field where she loves to assist patients and residents who are in need. Shonte published her first book, *Life is Challenging but Hang in There* in August 2015. Her story has become her ministry. She loves to write and plan events. Shonte has overcome many obstacles at an early age and has come out on top every time with the help of God. She is the C.E.O of the Cupcakes and Conversations Movement where she hosts events for dreamers and believers and inspire others to find their sweet spot. Shonte is also the founder of Daughters in Christ, where she helps women to be the best they can be with no excuses.

This year she received an award for outstanding author speaker and entrepreneur. Shonte was blessed with the best parents ever, the late Grace Monroe & Leon Monroe, a host of God parents and spiritual parents. Shonte has a sweet spot for people and never meets strangers. Her favorite quote is, "She believed she could do and She did."